W9-CRF-940

My Tall BOOK of Proverbs

Poems by
Donna Huisjen

Pictures by
Cindy Salans Rosenheim

Zonder**kidz**
The Children's Group of Zondervan Publishing House

To Amanda, Angela, and Khristina,
with love from Mom

Let love and faithfulness never leave you;
bind them around your neck, write them
on the tablet of your heart.
—Proverbs 3:3 (NIV)
D.H.

This collection of illustrations is dedicated to Nicky,
who brought them to life.
C.S.R.

My Tall Book of Proverbs: Favorite Proverbs in Rhyme
Text copyright © 1999 by Donna Huisjen
Illustrations copyright © 1999 by the Zondervan Corporation
ISBN 0-310-918626

Requests for information should be addressed to:

▟ ZondervanPublishingHouse
Mail Drop B20
Grand Rapids, Michigan 49530
http://www.zondervan.com

Library of Congress Catalog Card Number 98–61557

This edition printed on acid-free paper and meets the American National Standards Institute Z39.48 standard.

Illustrations by Cindy Salans Rosenheim

Printed in China

99 00 01 02 03/HK/ 10 9 8 7 6 5 4 3 2

This book belongs

to

_____

The Book of Proverbs

My grandma has a wooden doll.
She isn't tall or wide.
But when I pull the ends apart,
a smaller doll's inside.

Inside her is a tiny one.
That "nesting doll" is fun.
I always seem to be surprised
to find three dolls, not one!

The Bible is the Word of God.
It is our special guide.
But it is not one book—no,
it holds sixty-six inside!

One special book is Proverbs.
It tells us how to live.
Its wise words tell us how to love,
to share and to forgive.

Proverbs 3:3

Sometimes I tie a piece of string
around my finger; then
I can remember special things,
like *who*, *what*, *why*, or *when*.

The piece of string reminds me
that my mother (she's the *who*)
said, "Please be home by three o'clock."
(That's *what* and *when*.)

It's true she didn't tell me *why*,
but I will still obey.
Your Word, God, tells me to remember
love in just this way!

I think that I will make a love chain
from a piece of string.
That necklace will remind me
how I love you, O my King!

Proverbs 3:5–6

On the first day of school I got lost, God.
I forgot all the turns way too soon!
I remembered the way in the morning,
but the turns were all backward at noon!

My friend lives near school, on the same street.
There's no danger that she will get lost.
She just has to turn left from her driveway.
Then the crossing guard helps her to cross.

Your Word tells me that if I trust you,
you'll make the path straight for my feet.
I don't think I can move to my friend's house,
but I know that you'll be there to greet

me when my feet walk out of that building.
You will smile at me from where you stand.
Then we'll make all the right turns together—
you and me, step by step, hand in hand!

Proverbs 3:11–12

Sometimes I twist my brother's wrist
or yank my sister's hair.
What I get then is *discipline,*
like sitting in a chair.

Some people call it punishment,
but that is not quite true.
My parents won't just tell me, "*Don't!*"
They want to teach me, "*Do!*"

"Do what is right." "Do tell the truth."
"Do listen and obey."
If I forget, the consequences
help me see the way.

I wish that they would let me do
just what I want, and yet
I know that they just follow
the example that you set.

Proverbs 4:27

God, you say, "Keep your feet from evil."
I want to obey your Word now.
So I'll try to keep walking in good ways,
but I'm not at all sure I know how:

Squishy mud would leave stains on my
    church shoes.
I won't scamper barefoot in the snow.
If my boots are too small, they might pinch me.
A hornet could sting my big toe.

My feet sometimes do things when
    I'm angry—
things like kicking the wall—but they don't
do such things by themselves. They obey me,
and if I tell them not to, they won't.

At a circus I watched a man walking
on a tightrope high up in a tent.
So I point my toes straight on your pathway.
Now I think I know what your words meant!

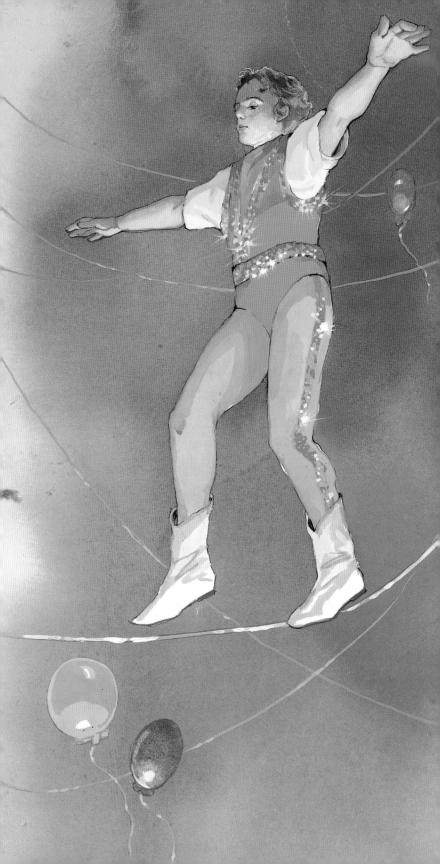

Proverbs 6:6–8

Last week, God, I went on a picnic—
just my mom and my best friend and me.
We rolled down a hill, floated sticks in a creek,
and ate sandwiches under a tree.

But when Mom said, "Let's pack up
   the food now,"
I suddenly felt hot and tired out!
I flopped on the grass, put my head
   on my arms,
kicked my feet hard and started to pout.

It was then that I looked up and saw him—
just an inch from the tip of my nose—
a little, black ant with a big crumb of cake,
big as one of my littlest toes!

First I laughed as he carried his treasure,
but, O God, in the Bible you say,
"Look at the wise ant, you can work too!"
So I knew I had better obey!

Proverbs 6:16–19

Your Word names the things that you hate, God.
There are seven things that you despise:
One is eyes that look proudly at others.
Two is mouths that are quick to tell lies.

Three is hands used to hit other kids, Lord.
Four is hearts that plan cruel tricks to play.
Five is feet that run fast to do evil.
Six is tongues that have mean things to say.

Seven is actions that break up two good
    friends.
God, I'd rather do things that you love,
that are good, kind and loving and thoughtful,
that will make you smile down from above.

I could pet *one* small puppy, smile *two* smiles,
share *three* cookies, or tell Dad *four* rhymes,
take *five* minutes to plan *six* surprises,
or kiss Mom on the cheek *seven* times!

Proverbs 6:20,22

When I was just a little kid,
before I started school,
my parents taught me of God's love
and of the Golden Rule.

I'm learning to treat others
like I want them to treat me,
to love God best, then to be kind
to everyone I see.

The Bible tells me that the things
I learned when I was small
will guide me as I walk through life,
so I won't slip and fall.

Oh, I might fall on slippery ice
or plop on soft beach sand,
but falling into sin is worse,
so God, please hold my hand!

Proverbs 11:13

I found a pair of slippers
in a shoe box—just Dad's size.
Mom said, "They're for his birthday.
Please don't tell—they're a surprise!"

I did try for awhile,
but they were all I thought about.
That secret tickled me inside—
I had to let it out!

I thought if I just whispered, Lord,
then it would be okay.
Dad said, "Please don't let Mom know
you told me this today."

I kept *Dad's* secret very well,
but God, I feel so bad
to know Dad had to *act* surprised
along with being glad!

Proverbs 12:10

I feel sorry for stray cats or kittens
people leave by the side of the road,
or a dog that has fleas but no collar,
or an old horse that carries a load.

Lord, my gerbil needs lots of fresh water,
soft clean bedding, a good apple treat,
hands for loving, long tubes for tunneling,
and a wheel for his quick, little feet.

Your Word tells me that a good person
cares for all of the creatures you've made.
But the kindest things some people do, God,
still aren't very kind, I'm afraid!

Please help me to treat people kindly
and love all the animals too.
May each word that I say and each action
be the best I can say or can do!

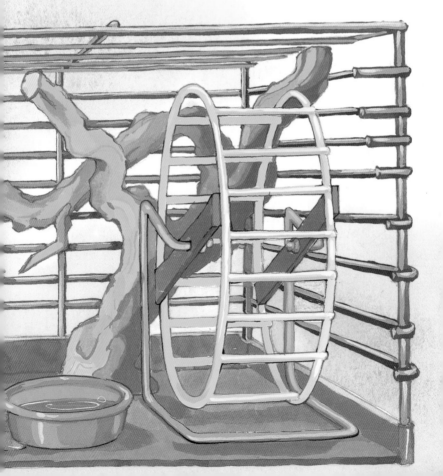

Proverbs 15:16–17

I'm not a vegetarian
who won't eat any meat.
And beets and cauliflower
aren't my favorite things to eat.

Mom says that they're good for me,
and so I eat a little bit.
She says that five bites are enough,
and then I get to quit!

But God, you say it's better
eating just a plate of peas
with words like, "Thank you very much"
and, "Pass the broccoli, please,"

than having a gigantic feast
with cake and ice cream too,
with looks and words and actions
that are angry, mean, or rude.

Proverbs 15:30

Last year I had my tonsils out.
At first I was afraid
of being sick so far from home.
But then my mother made

a game that made the time go fast.
Whenever someone came
into my room, I smiled and drew
a smile face for my game.

If they grinned back I drew
a matching smile face; it was fun.
I found that just one smile brings joy—
two smiles, more joy than one!

Before too long I found that smiles
are catching, like the flu.
The Bible says a happy look
makes people feel brand new!

Proverbs 15:32

Last night I got in trouble, God,
but you already know!
Dad sent me to my room to think,
but I refused to go.

Dad let me sit a little while,
then helped me to obey.
He took my hand and led me,
even though I knew the way.

I sulked and scowled and kicked my feet.
At first I didn't see
that I was not just mad at Dad.
No, I was mad at me!

The Bible says that if I hate
your discipline, then I
am really hurting me. You want
to teach me, so I'll try!

Proverbs 17:6

"Let me tell you about my grandchildren"
is a sticker I saw on a car.
And the way Grandma shows off my pictures
makes me feel like a grand movie star!

God says that children's children—
that's the same as a grandchild, like me—
are like gold crowns that sit upon white heads.
That's what makes me so grand, don't you see?

But what's special to Grandma and Grandpa
about me isn't what you might think.
They don't care if I'm smart or good-looking
or if I can skate fast on a rink.

No, the one thing that makes their eyes sparkle
and their kind faces crinkle in grins
is to know I love God—I'm a grandchild
who belongs to my grand, heavenly King!

Proverbs 17:17

My best friend likes me all the time.
She doesn't seem to care
if I am silly, sad, or mad
or if I'm playing fair.

She likes me when I'm sick or
when I'm acting like a pest.
She's better than a good friend, God,
that's why she is the best!

My little brother loves me too.
He stays close by my side.
And when the big kids pick on us,
he never runs and hides.

At first I found him hard to love—
I tried hard to pretend.
But sometimes now I think that
he was born to be my friend.

Proverbs 17:22

The lady who lives next to me
has white hair and a cane.
Mom says she looks so sad because
she's in a lot of pain.

Today I stopped to talk to her.
I sang some songs and said
a silly rhyme my mother likes
to read to me in bed.

We laughed and laughed so hard
that we both started to cry tears!
She said, "I haven't laughed so much
or felt so good in years!"

The Bible says a cheerful heart's
a kind of medicine.
It might not make you well,
but it's a good place to begin!

Proverbs 17:27–28

Sometimes when I get angry, God,
I stomp and scowl and shout.
Then everyone around me knows
what I'm so mad about.

I *lose* my temper; then I *lose*
some more things, you'll agree—
my friends, my cool, my self-respect
(that's what I think of me)!

Your Word says I'd be smarter just
to *keep* my mouth zipped shut—
to *keep* my temper, *keep* the peace,
and *keep* the devil out.

If *losers*, God, are weepers,
then I won't make a peep.
To be a "finder–*keep*er," I'll
remember what to *keep*!

Proverbs 18:17

My mom says she wants to hear both sides
when my brother and I have a fight.
If just one of us tells her the story,
she can't tell who's wrong or who's right.

My brother and I both have memories.
Those memories remember just fine.
But mine only wants to remember
the half of the story that's mine!

When Mom starts to ask me some questions,
I start to think back, "Oop's, that's right!
I guess I punched him first in the stomach,
but he teased me and started the fight!"

My conscience helps me to remember—
that's your voice I hear in my heart—
that the best way to end a big fight, God,
is to stop it before it can start!

Proverbs 19:17

I wish, dear God, that I
could give a big surprise to you—
a crinkly, sparkly package,
with bright red ribbons too!

At church I put a dollar
in the basket every time.
But it is really from my parents—
I don't give a dime.

My prayers and songs and praises
are a kind of gift, that's true.
But I want something really special
just from me to you!

O Lord, you have an answer:
When I share a treat or toy
with someone else who needs it—
then, God, I bring you joy!

Proverbs 20:11-12

I have a reputation
that goes with me every day.
It means that those who know me
know I'll act a certain way.

My friends know if they tease me
just how fast I will get mad,
or whether I will tell the truth
or what might make me sad.

I want to be trustworthy
even when no one's in sight.
I sometimes do stuff wrong but try
my best to do stuff right.

You gave me ears to hear and eyes
to see what's right or wrong.
But when I have to choose, O Lord,
please make me sure and strong.

Proverbs 20:22

When the neighbor boy trips me and teases,
I yell, "I'll pay you back—just you wait!"
Lord, your Word tells me not to get even,
but sometimes I remember too late.

Even though he was wrong I could laugh too.
I could say, "You just wait for your turn!"
If I'm smiling the words sound much kinder.
I think now I'm beginning to learn!

You tell me that I should just wait, God,
because you will take care of what's wrong.
It not my job to punish my friends, Lord.
That's your business and you're wise
    and strong!

Sometimes kids can be mean, but my dad says,
"Let it go. Two wrongs don't make a right."
Making them lose won't make me a winner,
but trying to win a friend might!

Proverbs 22:1

The Bible tells me of a jewel
that sparkles more than gold.
A good name is the greatest treasure
I could ever hold!

I like my first name pretty well.
The middle's okay too.
I have the very same last name
that both my brothers do.

But that is not the kind of name
that you, God, care about.
No, "God's child" tells the world
just who I am from inside out.

Lord, help me find that gem that glitters
for the world to see.
When people hear the name "God's child,"
please help them know it's me!

Proverbs 22:6

The Bible makes a promise
to my parents. They are told
that if they train me in God's ways
I'll love him when I'm old.

My mom and dad have parents, too,
who taught them years ago
and showed them by their lives
how God's love could make them grow.

My mom and dad can *tell* me
what to do, and that's okay.
I'd rather have them *show* me
how to live for God each day.

I like to be a copycat,
and this is how I know
why teachers have a *Show* and *Tell*
and not a *Tell* and *Show*.

Proverbs 25:14

Sometimes when I've been running
on a sticky summer day,
I wish a cooling rain would come
to chase the heat away.

The clouds grow black, the thunder growls,
and lightning flashes white.
But then the clouds just spit at me
before the sky turns bright!

The sunshine pushes with its rays—
the dark sky rolls away.
And once again I'm playing
on a hot and sweaty day.

The clouds that don't bring rain
are like the promises I make.
But then when I don't keep my word,
my friends know it was fake.

Proverbs 26:20

Our fireplace is special.
When it's cold, Dad lights a fire.
He starts it with some kindling wood,
then stacks the logs up higher.

At first the flames dance high and orange.
But in a little while,
they dance a little lower,
so Dad adds logs to the pile.

My family loves each other,
but still sometimes we fight,
with tempers that are hot like fire,
we stomp and yell, "I'm right!"

If we don't add more fuel—
if we don't mumble, scowl, or pout—
the angry flames will soon die down.
They'll flicker and go out!

Proverbs 27:2

Oh, I know I'm a pretty good reader!
I can dance and turn somersaults too.
I can stand on my head if you help me,
so I see with an upside-down view!

I can color a beautiful picture,
skate on roller blades, hit a ball too.
I'll count backwards out loud if you ask me—
these are some of the things I can do!

It's okay that I feel good about me,
but it isn't all right if I boast.
For I know every kid's good at some things,
but nobody can be good at most!

Lord, I'm happy that I have these talents,
but the praises should not come from me.
All the things I can do are your gifts, God.
Let me just be the best I can be!

Proverbs 27:15

Sometimes a dripping faucet,
when I'm lying in my bed,
will wake me up, like when a song
gets stuck inside my head.

Sounds that repeat can comfort me,
like crickets, waves, and laughs.
But other noises bother me,
like hiccups, sniffs, and coughs.

The Bible says that quarreling—
the kind that just won't stop—
is like the drip–drop-drip when
rain plip–plops from my rooftop.

"It's mine!" "I had it first!" "No, mine!"
"Nuh-uh!" "Uh-huh!" "No way!"
One simple word, "okay," can
make the fight go away!

Proverbs 27:19

In our big hallway mirror
I can take a look at me,
pretending that I've never met
the someone that I see.

But my reflection only shows
my outside, and I know
that there's so much within me
that the mirror doesn't show.

Your Word, God, tells me that my heart's
a kind of mirror too!
My friends can see what's inside
by the things I say and do.

The mirror tells a lot about
my outside, but I'm awed
to know when people see my love,
they see a child of God!

Proverbs 30:8–9

I wish that I were richer, God.
I just don't have enough.
In order to be happy, well—
I think I need more stuff!

But you say I have plenty, Lord,
that it's not good to be
too rich—I'll think that I'm in charge—
or poor, and I agree!

You say that I need daily bread.
I like white bread—wheat too,
and bagels, biscuits, crazy bread—
but God, just bread just won't do!

My mom says "bread" means what I *need*—
some *wants* might not get met.
You give me everything I need.
I'm glad for what I get!

Proverbs 31:10–31

The Bible says a lady who
loves God and family too
is better than a chest of rubies;
I know her—do you?

She sounds like someone special
who makes lunches when it's dark.
She sets out clothes, signs notes for school,
does lots of other work.

She holds my baby sister
in her left arm. With her right
she pours my milk, then with her
shoulder switches on the light.

Both arms are free for bear hugs
when I leave, though, just the same.
Her goodness makes her beautiful—
I'm glad "Mom" is her name!

My Tall Book of Proverbs
Favorite Proverbs in Rhyme

Donna Huisjen *lives in Grand Rapids, MI, and is the single adoptive parent of three daughters, ages 13, 17, and 21. A graduate of Calvin College in Grand Rapids, Ms. Huisjen is an editorial assistant at Zondervan Publishing House.*

Cindy Salans Rosenheim *is a graduate of Tufts University in Medford, MA. Ms. Rosenheim has been an illustrator for more than twenty years, specializing in children's illustration and design. She lives with her husband and their three sons in San Francisco, CA.*

Editorial by **Ruth A. DeJager**
Art Direction & Design by **Jody Langley**